Clothing, Costumes, and Uniforms Throughout American History™

What People Wore During the Civil War

∞ Allison Stark Draper ∞

The Rosen Publishing Group's
PowerKids Press™
New York

For my mother

Published in 2001 by The Rosen Publishing Group, Inc.
29 East 21st Street, New York, NY 10010

First Edition

Book Design: Emily Muschinske

Photo Credits: Photo reenactments on pp. 3, 4, 5, 8, 9, 11, 13, 14, 15, 18, 19, 22 © Jeffrey Foxx; pp. 5, 6, 10, 11, 20, 21 © Bettmann/CORBIS; pp. 7, 9,17 © CORBIS; map illustration on p. 7 © Emily Muschinske; p.12 © Medford Historical Society Collection/CORBIS; p.16 © SuperStock.

Draper, Allison Stark.
    What people wore during the Civil War / Allison Stark Draper.
        p. cm.— (Clothing, costumes, and uniforms throughout American history)
    Summary: This book describes what people wore in the days of the Civil War, discussing Union and Confederate uniforms, women and children's clothes, and slaves' clothes.
    ISBN 0-8239-5669-5
    1. Costume—United States—History—19th century—Juvenile literature. 2. United States—History—Civil War, 1861-1865—Juvenile literature. 3. United States—Social life and customs—19th century—Juvenile literature. [1. Costume—History—19th century. 2. United States—Social life and customs—19th century. 3. United States—History—Civil War, 1861-1865.] I. Title. II. Series.

GT610 .D73 2000
391'.00973—dc21   00-036713

Manufactured in the United States of America

Contents

Clothes of a Changing Nation

By the 1860s, the United States was much different from what it had been at its birth nearly 100 years before. There were many **immigrants** living in the North. A lot of these immigrants worked in factories. Wealthy Northerners owned the factories. People in the South made their money growing cotton on **plantations**.

Rich people in the United States dressed like Europeans. Men wore bright white shirts and frock coats. A frock coat fit tightly around the shoulders and chest. It was loose below the waist. A frock

Women wore simple skirts, called petticoats, under their dresses. They also wore underclothes called breeches that came down to the knee.

coat was long, ending at a man's knees. Wealthy women wore huge dresses with hoop skirts underneath. A hoop skirt was made of wire and shaped like a bell. Poor women who worked in factories wore plain skirts. Hoop skirts cost too much and might get caught in a machine.

Hoop skirts were not comfortable to wear. The picture above shows a woman being helped into the bell-shaped hoop.

The South Secedes

Plantation owners used slaves to work their cotton fields. The slaves were **kidnapped** from Africa. Slaves were considered property and were not paid. Slaves worked as dressmakers and weavers, but did not have their own nice clothes. Many slave owners would give their male slaves just one shirt and suit per year. Northerners thought owning slaves was **cruel** and wanted to end slavery. The plantation owners thought they would lose their farms without slaves to work for free. The South decided to **secede** from the United States. They called themselves the Confederate States of America. The North was called the Union.

This is a ship that brought slaves who were kidnapped from Africa to the United States.

6

These men were slaves who escaped to the North to be free. Many runaway slaves could not afford to buy new clothes. The man in the back did not even have shoes.

Union

Border States

Confederacy

People living in states known as border states were split in their opinions about slavery.

7

The Blue and the Gray

In 1861, Abraham Lincoln became the president of the United States. Lincoln thought that it was important for the country to stay **united**. He also thought that slavery was very cruel. The North and South could not agree. This disagreement started the Civil War. When the North and the South went to war, the uniforms of the two forces were very much alike. The only difference in the uniforms was the colors. The North wore blue wool uniforms. This was the color of the United States Army. The soldiers from the South wore gray uniforms because they already had these uniforms from their local **militias**.

Confederate soldiers wore gray wool uniforms.

Union soldiers had to carry a lot of equipment. This man is carrying a tin cup and a canteen. Canteens are small containers made of wood, metal, or animal skin that hold water.

canteen

Soldiers wore pocket watches that attached to their uniforms with a chain.

These men fought for the Union army. Their uniforms were made of blue wool. In the summer, these heavy uniforms made the soldiers very hot and sweaty.

Homemade Uniforms

Most of the land in the South was farmland. Unlike up North, the South did not have many machines to make uniforms. As the war went on, the South ran out of money to buy uniforms. Northern soldiers also made it hard for the South to get uniforms. This was because the Northern soldiers blocked the **routes** the South used for trade. Some Southern soldiers had the money to buy their own wool uniforms. However, many did not. By the middle of the war, many Southern soldiers had to wear their regular clothes. They dyed them gray to match the other soldiers' uniforms. When they ran out of gray dye, Southern soldiers would use yellow dye.

Southern women made uniforms by hand or by using an early type of sewing machine.

Southern soldiers dyed their clothes gray to match the army's uniform. When they ran out of gray dye, they used yellow.

In the South, slaves worked on farmland like this cotton plantation near the Mississippi River.

Do Not Dress in Blue

The North had more money and supplies than the South. The clothing factories were in the North. When Southerners won battles against the North, they would take clothes from the bodies of dead soldiers. At first the Southerners tried to boil the blue dye out of the clothes. Later it became too much trouble for them to boil the clothes. The Southern soldiers began wearing the blue uniforms. This was dangerous for soldiers on both sides. They could not tell their own men from the enemy since both were wearing blue uniforms. In 1864, the Northern army warned the Southern soldiers to stop wearing blue uniforms. Any Southern soldier caught wearing a blue uniform would be put to death.

Some women stayed near the battlefield during the Civil War. They washed clothes and took care of injured soldiers. They also boiled the blue dye out of uniforms that the Southern soldiers stole from the dead bodies of Union soldiers.

By wearing the blue uniforms of the North, Southern soldiers risked being shot at by a Southerner mistaking them for a Union soldier. Northern soldiers would think that a man in blue was on his side. He might get an awful surprise when the soldier turned out to be an enemy from the South.

Dresses for Day and Night

When the Civil War started, both sides thought it would end quickly. Rich women continued to visit with each other and have parties. A rich woman changed her clothes a few times a day. She wore a day dress when she was eating breakfast or doing work around the house. Day dresses had narrow sleeves. This was so the sleeves would not fall into a pot of soup or get caught in a piece of needlepoint.

An afternoon dress had more decoration on it than a day dress did. It had fuller sleeves. These dresses were made of silk or fine wool. Evening dresses had short sleeves and low necks. They were decorated with lace, ribbons, and feathers.

Afternoon dresses were made of fancy material like silk and decorated with stitching and bows.

This woman's bag is made out of pieces of carpet. During the war, people were careful not to waste any material. Many carpet bags had locks on them to protect a woman's belongings.

Glasses were round, oval, or rectangular and made out of metal. The arms of the glasses were straight. They did not bend around the ear.

Southern women often carried a fan to use in hot weather. Sometimes the fans were made from sandalwood, which gave off a nice smell.

15

Beauty and Pain

At the time of the Civil War, women's dresses had very small waists. A tiny waist was thought to be a sign of beauty on a woman. A woman would make her waist smaller by tightening her **corset**. Corsets were worn around the middle part of a woman's body. They laced up in the back. A woman would have her sisters or **servants** pull the corset tight around her body. Doctors believed that it  was unhealthy for a woman to wear a tight corset. They warned that tight corsets could crush a woman's lungs. The corsets made it hard for women to breathe. Women often fainted. Many women carried **smelling salts** so someone could wake them up if they fainted from wearing a tight corset.

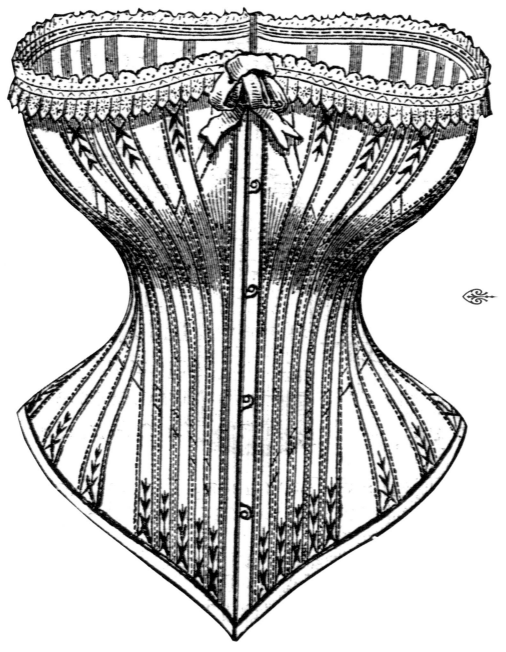

Corsets were made to squeeze a woman's waist so that it looked small. Sometimes a woman would pull the corset so tight that it became hard for her to breathe.

Not in Uniform

In the 1860s, men who were not fighting in the war wore long, narrow trousers. They also wore **waistcoats** and stiff, white shirts. Sometimes they wore fake shirtfronts called **dickeys**. Dickeys were the size of the part of the shirt that showed underneath the waistcoat. They were easier to clean than a whole shirt. Under a waistcoat, dickeys looked like regular shirts. Men wore frock coats. They wore tall, silk hats in dark colors. They carried large watches on chains. These chains fit into special watch pockets. Working men wore boots and sturdy wool pants. They also wore shirts that buttoned only halfway down their chests.

During the Civil War, many men wore beards, mustaches, or both. This man is also wearing a pocket watch.

During the Civil War, working people could not buy new clothes very often. This boy's work boots are worn down.

This boy is wearing a shirt that buttons halfway down his chest. Working boys wore hats with a wide brim to protect them from the sun.

Dressing Like Grown-Ups

Boys and girls dressed alike until they were about six years old. They wore both brightly colored and white gowns. Boys sometimes wore skeleton suits. These suits were made up of a shirt and a pair of pants that had buttons all around the waist. It had **seams** that could be let out when the boy got bigger.

When children turned six, they started dressing like adults. In rich families, boys wore velvet suits and silk stockings. Girls wore ruffled **pantaloons** and hoop skirts. In poorer families, boys wore shirts made out of **muslin**. Girls wore dresses made out of cotton, muslin, or **calico**.

As children got older, they began to dress more like adults. This girl has on a dress with a full skirt and puffy sleeves.

These Northern schoolchildren wore clothes made out of plain cloth like cotton, muslin, or wool. Girls parted their hair in the middle, while boys parted their hair on the side.

Remembering Loved Ones

Women often wore jewelry that reminded them of people close to them. A woman might wear a piece of jewelry called a cameo that had the carving of the face of a loved one on it. A cameo is a piece of carved stone or shell that is usually an off-white color. The cameo is sometimes set against a different-colored background. Women also wore jewelry made out of hair. They took a lock of hair from a loved one. Then they braided the hair to make bracelets or key chains. Sometimes a jeweler would form the hair into the shape of a flower or **landscape**. The jeweler would glue the piece to a white background to make a pin.

The pin on the left uses hair to form the shape of a flower.

This pin on the right shows a photograph of a loved one.

Glossary

calico (KA-lih-koh) Cotton fabric printed with small designs.

corset (KOR-sit) An undergarment worn around the middle of the body that is tightened with laces.

cruel (KROOL) Causing pain or suffering.

dickeys (DIK-eez) Fake shirt fronts that are worn under waistcoats.

immigrants (IH-muh-grints) People who move to a new country from another country.

kidnapped (KID-napt) Carried off by force.

landscape (LAND-skayp) A view of scenery on land.

militias (muh-LIH-shuhs) Groups of people who are trained and ready to fight, but who are not in the army.

muslin (MUZ-lin) A cotton fabric.

pantaloons (PANT-uh-loonz) Close-fitting pants that are usually shorter than ankle length.

plantations (plan-TAY-shunz) Large farms on which cotton, tobacco, and sugarcane are grown.

routes (ROOTS) The paths you take to get somewhere.

seams (SEEMZ) The lines formed by sewing together two pieces of cloth.

secede (suh-SEED) To withdraw from a group or country.

servants (SER-ventz) People who are paid to work in a household.

smelling salts (SMEL-ing SALTZ) Strong-smelling chemicals that can wake a person up when he or she faints.

united (yoo-NY-ted) Joined together to act as a single group.

waistcoats (WAYST-koats) Vests that are worn over a man's shirt and under his coat.

Index

Web Sites

To learn more about what people wore during the Civil War, check out these Web sites:

http://hometown.aol.com/b7vainf/reenacting.html
http://www.thehistorynet.com/THNarchives/CivilWar

24